# The Little Flower

## A Parable of Saint Thérèse of Lisieux

Text by Becky Arganbright
Illustrations by Tracey Arvidson

**Our Sunday Visitor**
Huntington, Indiana
www.osv.com

*The Little Flower: A Parable of Saint Thérèse of Lisieux*

24 23 22 21 20 19    3 4 5 6 7 8 9

ISBN: 978-1-68192-498-4 (Inventory No. T2387)
LCCN: 2019939998

PRINTED IN THE UNITED STATES OF AMERICA

Our Sunday Visitor Publishing Division
Our Sunday Visitor, Inc.
200 Noll Plaza
Huntington, IN  46750
1-800-348-2440

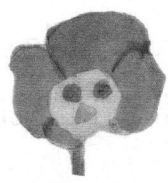

*If a little flower could speak,*
*it seems to me that it would tell us*
*quite simply all that God has done for it,*
*without hiding any of its gifts.*
—St. Thérèse of Lisieux

I would like to dedicate this book to all
who have encouraged me, especially my prayer buddies:
Mom, Tamara, Leila and Jamie!
Thank you for your prayers and encouragement!

And most importantly, to St. Thérèse,
who has laid out her "Little Way"
making it easy for the rest of us to follow.
—B.A.

Dedicated to our loving Heavenly Father, who faithfully cares for us daily.
—T.A.

Once upon a time, there lived a little girl
named Thérèse Martin who lived in Lisieux, France.

Thérèse loved Jesus very much.
She loved Him not just a little bit,
but with all her heart!
Loving God made Thérèse happy.

However, Thérèse was very young.
She knew that because she was little,
she could not do big things for Jesus.

She could not travel to far-off lands
to tell people about Jesus.
She could not serve the poor like the great saints.
And she could not be like her older sisters
who went away to the Carmelite convent,
spending their days in prayer.

Thérèse wanted to do great things for Jesus, too.
But how could someone little do great things?

Jesus often spoke to Thérèse's heart,
and one day, He answered her question
by telling her the story of a little flower.

There was once a garden full of many flowers.

Everyone who passed by the garden stopped
to admire their bright colors and fragrant smells.

The Gardener was pleased that the flowers
made people happy. He was glad to share
their beautiful colors and fragrances
with anyone who wanted to enjoy the garden.

There were other flowers in the garden as well.
But unlike the roses and lilies, these flowers were small
and ordinary: buttercups and bluebells,
daisies and daffodils, periwinkle and primroses and pansies.

These flowers were so small and ordinary,
people often passed by without even noticing them.

This made one
particular flower,
Pansy, very sad.

When the Gardner saw how sad Pansy was,
he knelt down beside her.

"Why are you so sad, my little Pansy?" he asked.

"Oh, Master!" cried Pansy. "Everyone comes into the garden
to admire the big flowers. But little flowers like me are too
small and ordinary. What good are little flowers if no one
notices us?"

The Gardener smiled. "It is true that the world notices
the big flowers. That is why I planted them,
so their splendor might draw people to the garden."

The Gardner gently lifted a petal of Pansy's sad face.
"But little Pansy, it is not true that no one notices you!
When I kneel to till the soil, what do you think I see?"

"What?" the little flower asked.

The Gardner leaned very close to Pansy
and whispered, "I see you."

"When I sit in my garden and curl my toes in the warmth
of the soil, I see all my little flowers scattered upon the earth
in bright and cheerful colors.

It is the beauty of my small
and simple flowers that
makes me smile.

And someday,
my little flower,
those who rest
in my garden
will notice you, too."

Pansy understood. She might be little,
but she could be as beautiful as the lily or the rose
in her own little way. She might be little,
but that did not make her any less important
to the Gardener.

Thérèse understood, too.
You see, the Gardener in the story represents Jesus;
the flowers are His friends;
and the garden is His Church.
And who do you think the little flower is?

Yes, the little flower is Thérèse!

Thérèse came to understand that, like the flowers,
some people serve God in big ways, and some people
serve God in little ways. Even someone little
is beautiful to Jesus, and even someone
who serves God in little ways
can make Him smile.

Thérèse felt that God was calling her
to be little, just like Pansy. And from that moment on,
Thérèse nicknamed herself "the Little Flower."

Her way of serving God would be little,
just like Pansy . . .

. . . but her little way would be done with GREAT love!

## About Saint Thérèse

Thérèse Martin was born in France on January 2, 1873, the last of nine children, four of whom died in infancy. After losing her mother to breast cancer at the age of four, Thérèse became a very sensitive child, crying over almost anything. Her sensitive nature caused a great deal of suffering for her. But under the loving guidance of her father and four older sisters, she grew in holiness and wisdom far beyond her years.

By May 1887, Thérèse was determined to enter the Carmelite community at Lisieux, even though she was only fourteen. When she announced this desire to her father, he picked a small white flower, roots intact, and handed it to her, explaining how God had brought it into being and cared for it to that moment. St. Thérèse later said that as she listened to her father, she believed the flower was a symbol of her own story.

After overcoming objections from Church officials over her young age, the fifteen-year-old

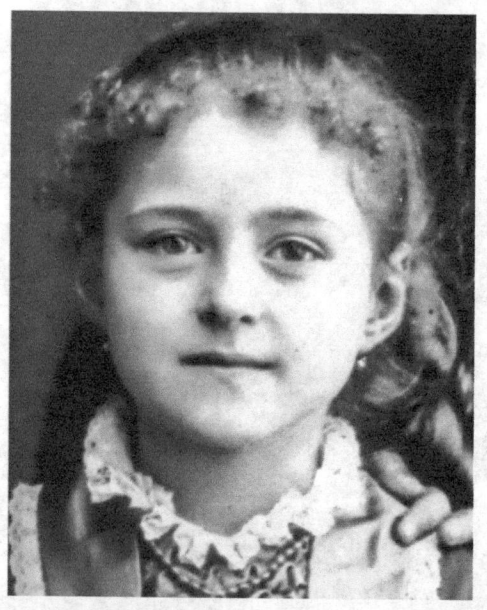

Thérèse entered the Carmelite community at Lisieux, where she would live for the rest of her life with three of her sisters who also became Carmelite nuns (another sister became a Visitation nun). Over the remaining nine years of her life there, Thérèse blossomed in strength and holiness. In 1895, she was ordered to write a memoir of her childhood; this, together with some of her other writings, was published after her death as *Story of a Soul.* She died of tuberculosis in 1897 at the age of twenty-four.

*Story of a Soul* quickly became one of the most popular spiritual writings of the twentieth century. Despite its apparent simplicity, many have found in it a profound wisdom, so much so that Pope John Paul II declared Thérèse a Doctor of the Church, one of only four women so named. One of her most important insights was her discovery of "the Little Way" of humility and child-like dependence on God: "I rejoice to be little because only children, and those who are like them, will be admitted to the heavenly banquet," she wrote. The image of "the little flower" became a symbol not only of herself, but of her spiritual way. She refers to this image so often in her autobiography that to this day that she is famously known as "The Little Flower."

In *Story of a Soul,* Thérèse writes:

*Jesus set before me the book of nature; I understood how all the flowers He has created are beautiful, how the splendor of the rose and the whiteness of the lily do not take away the perfume of the little violet or the delightful simplicity of the daisy. I understood that if all flowers wanted to be roses, nature would lose her springtime beauty, and the fields would no longer be decked out with little wild flowers.*

*And so it is in the world of souls, Jesus' garden. He willed to create great souls comparable to lilies and roses, but He has created smaller ones and these must be content to be daisies or violets destined to give joy to God's glances when He looks down at His feet. Perfection consists in doing His will, in being what He wills us to be.*

Thérèse de Lisieux, *Story of a Soul: The Autobiography of St. Thérèse of Lisieux,* Third Edition (Washington: ICS Publications, 1996), page 14. Translated by John Clarke.